Buying Gemstones and Jewellery in
MYANMAR
(Burma)

First Edition

Kim Rix GG (GIA)

Published by
Filament Publishing Ltd
16, Croydon Road, Waddon, Croydon,
Surrey, CR0 4PA, United Kingdom
Telephone +44 (0)20 8688 2598
Fax +44 (0)20 7183 7186
info@filamentpublishing.com
www.filamentpublishing.com

© Kim Rix 2022

The right of Kim Rix to be identified as the author of this work
has been asserted by her in accordance with the
Designs and Copyright Act 1988.

ISBN 978-1-913623-94-4

Printed by PrintGuy

This book is subject to international copyright and may not be copied
in any way without the prior written permission of the publishers.

Foreword

Myanmar (formerly Burma) is a gateway into Association of South-East Asian Nations (ASEAN) countries such as China and India, which have the biggest populations in the world and large gemstone markets. Myanmar is rich in natural resources: you can find the best rubies in the world here (pigeon blood) and its sapphire is famed for its exceptionally high quality. The country provides the largest volume of the highest quality jadeite in the world.

However Myanmar was, for over 50 years, under the control of a military government which failed to recognise the importance of supply chain development in the gem and jewellery industry. Hence the country has had limited opportunities to promote its products globally.

Therefore, Ms Rix's encouragement, in this *Gemstone Detective* book, to purchase gemstones is a true honour. She offers insight on why travellers should buy gemstones in Myanmar and offers considerable evidence-based information on how to do this.

In conclusion, I believe Ms Rix's book shows inside knowledge of Myanmar's gemstone industry, which will help its development into the global market.

Dr Aung Kyaw Win
Vice-President
Myanmar Gems & Jewelry Entrepreneurs' Association (MGJEA)

Top Sone Jewellery Workshop © *Kim Rix*

Contents

Introduction — 7
- Why you need this book — 9
- What makes me an expert? — 12
- Don't learn the hard way! — 12

Buying gemstones in Myanmar — 17
- About Burmese jade — 19
- Burmese jade: knowing what you're looking at — 21
- About Burmese ruby — 28
- About Burmese sapphire — 31
- Ruby and sapphire: knowing what you're looking at — 33
- Other gemstones found in Myanmar — 39
- Spotting a fake — 55
- Buying in Myanmar: three things you need to know — 57
- Deciding what you want — 59
- Choosing where to buy — 61
- Q&A's — 65
- At a glance tips — 66

Reputable traders in Myanmar — 67
- Yangon — 69
- Mandalay — 81
- Mogok — 92

Essential Information — 109
- Visas and permits — 111
- Certificates of authenticity and grading reports — 113
- Prices — what to expect — 118
- Gemstones as investments — 119
- The ethics of buying gemstones — 120

Appendices — 121
- Glossary — 122
- Acknowledgements — 125
- About the author — 126
- Disclaimer — 126
- Connect with Kim — 127

Tourmaline Scorpion brooch © Kim Rix

INTRODUCTION

Visit Chan Thar Gyi Pagoda to see old jewellery donated by the local people
© Kim Rix

INTRODUCTION

Why you need this book

This book is an essential beginner's guide to gemstones in Myanmar (formerly Burma), whether you are looking to buy or simply learn more about them. It is a 'how to' manual for tourists, from gemstone enthusiasts and jewellers to those with little knowledge about gemstones. I have written it to introduce you to Myanmar's gemstone industry and to help guide you to making the right buying decision.

With the tourist industry still in its infancy, Myanmar is one of the few places a visitor can have a truly authentic experience. There is so much on offer here – stunning scenery, gourmet food, the famous gem markets and a plethora of breathtaking temples and pagodas, encrusted with gold and jewels.

Myanmar is legendary for its beautiful gemstones and I want you to experience this fascinating country equipped with some essential knowledge and a large helping of confidence. Whether you are hoping to treat yourself to an extra-special souvenir of your latest adventure or travelling to learn more about the gemstone industry, what could be more exciting than buying your gemstone in the very country whose earth formed it?

I want to share, in a simple and positive way, my experience and knowledge – *inside* knowledge that you won't easily find by yourself. I want you to feel confident about buying a gemstone in a foreign country, and I want you to have a good experience doing so.

The Internet is awash with confusing and out of date information. It's very hard to find everything you really need to know – all the tips and tricks to help you avoid the pitfalls.

www.gemstonedetective.com

INTRODUCTION

This book will give you the vital information you need before making your purchase. In it, I disclose what the travel guidebooks and websites don't tell you.

I'll reveal:

Who to trust
What to look for
When to walk away
Where to buy
Why you need to be sure

Jade necklace © Kim Rix

What makes me an expert?

It has taken a lot of travel and a few calculated risks to gain the knowledge I'm going to share with you. Everything in this book is based on personal experience and local expertise.

The letters after my name are testament to my knowledge. I'm a gemmologist with qualifications from the GIA (Gemological Institute of America) – the world's leading authority on gemstones. However, it's my extensive global travel and research that will make this book so useful to you.

My list of friends and genuinely reliable contacts around the world is now large enough to enable me to get in amongst the hustle and bustle of the global gem-trading community to bring you the best local tips for buying in many different countries.

I also hope that writing this book will boost Myanmar's small gem-trading businesses: the exceptionally hard-working miners, dealers and jewellers who, like all of us, are trying to make a living in challenging times.

Don't learn the hard way!

This book is not about buying discount gemstones. As you'll learn, Myanmar is not somewhere you will find cheap bargains. However, this book will help you to make an informed decision about what and where to buy. It will give you the knowledge needed to feel comfortable that your purchase is genuine and therefore make the whole experience fun and memorable for the right reasons.

INTRODUCTION

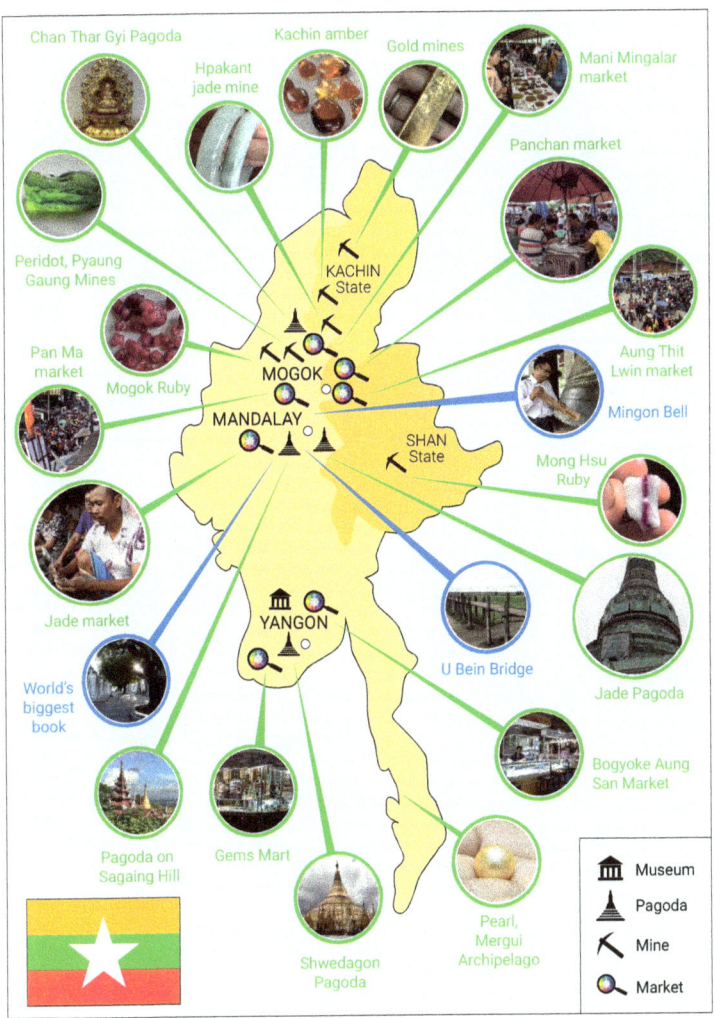

Werawsana Pagoda, Mandalay (jade pagoda) © Kim Rix

INTRODUCTION

A gemstone-studded peacock made by Silver Sky Handicrafts © Kim Rix

BUYING GEMSTONES IN MYANMAR

Looking at black jade © Kim Rix

About Burmese jade

Myanmar is rich in gemstones of many varieties, but the country is most famous for its jade, ruby and sapphire. Note that, though Burma is now known as Myanmar, the industry still refers to the country's jade, ruby and sapphire as 'Burmese'.

Many people are unaware that the term 'jade' actually refers to two different types of mineral: jadeite and nephrite. Jadeite is the more valuable of the two and differs from nephrite in range of colour, rarity and hardness (jadeite measures 6.5-7 on the Mohs scale; nephrite 6.5-6). Whereas nephrite occurs in a relatively limited range of colours (dark green, white and black) jadeite's spectrum encompasses not only those colours, but also shades of red, yellow, orange, lavender, blue and brown. Of all jadeite's colours, the most prized is a vivid, emerald green. Nephrite is mined in many countries around the world, but jadeite is found in only 10, with Myanmar producing nearly all of the world's finest jadeite gemstones.

From now on in this guide, I'll be using the name jade to refer to Burmese jadeite unless I mention otherwise.

Marking up the jade to cut © Kim Rix

Myanmar's biggest jade mines are in Kachin state, in the north of the country. The Hpakan-Tawmaw jade tract is known locally as Kyaukseinmyo, which means 'Jade Land' – an appropriate name for an area that produces most of the world's supply of jade. The mines here sometimes yield stones of exceptional size. In 2016, a jade stone weighing 175 tonnes was uncovered – a find worth an estimated $170m (£140m).

It is important to say here that a great deal of controversy, both humanitarian and environmental, surrounds Myanmar's jade industry. In the same way that we need to become wise to the subject of so-called 'Blood' (or 'Conflict') diamonds, we should also educate ourselves on the issues of Burmese jade.

Werawsana, the world's first jade Pagoda © *Kim Rix*

Burmese jade: knowing what you're looking at

Jade is valued according to several factors, the most important being colour, translucency and texture. Clarity, cut and size are also considered. Note that the size of jade is frequently measured in millimetres rather than by carat weight. Again, taste is personal and you may find certain stones more attractive than others, even if the market values them less highly. What you want to avoid is paying more than market value for a stone because a canny seller has taken advantage of your ignorance.

Colour
As is the case for almost all gemstones, colour is the most important factor when valuing a piece of jade. Let's take a look at the different aspects of colour that relate to jade: hue, saturation, tone and distribution.

Hue
Though jade occurs in a variety of colours, a vivid emerald green with no hints of any other colour is the most prized and consequently attracts the highest prices. After this come other bright shades of green: the slightly less vivid 'kingfisher' green and the more yellow 'apple' green, for example. Note that the precise boundaries between these hues are not universally agreed: one person's kingfisher green may be another's emerald green. Lavender-coloured jade is also highly valued.

Saturation
Generally, highly saturated jade is the most valuable. This is especially the case with hues of green and lavender. High saturation means that the hue will appear intense, even from a distance.

Tone

The most valuable jade gemstones have a medium tone: neither too dark, nor too light.

Distribution

A uniform distribution of colour within a jade gemstone fetches the highest prices. Patchy stones are generally less valuable. Note, however, that some stones have colour distributions that are highly prized – 'moss-in-snow' jade, for example, which has veins of green within a white background.

Translucency

The translucency (or transparency) of a gem refers to how much light is able to pass through the stone. A transparent object allows all light to pass through; a translucent object some light; an opaque object no light. Jade ranges from translucent (or semi-transparent) to completely opaque, and stones with high translucency are the most valuable.

Top Tip: check the translucency of black jade by shining a torch through it – if it appears green, that's a sign of good quality.

Texture

Closely related to translucency, the texture of jade refers to the composition of grains (interlocking micro crystals) within the body of the gemstone. Jade with a coarse texture will appear dull and dry, whereas jade with a fine texture will appear lustrous (i.e. bright and glossy). The texture of a piece of jade is sometimes referred to as 'old mine' (fine), 'relatively old mine' (medium) and 'new mine' (coarse).

Clarity

The finest jade is free of inclusions, which affect the colour and translucency of the gemstone. Dark inclusions detract from value more than light-coloured ones, and visible black inclusions are especially problematic in the Chinese market, as black is considered an unlucky colour there. Certain inclusions can be considered beautiful.

Of other factors affecting clarity, fractures and fissures will more seriously detract from jade's value than inclusions – not only because they are unsightly, but because jade has significance in its main market, China, as a stone of longevity and strength.

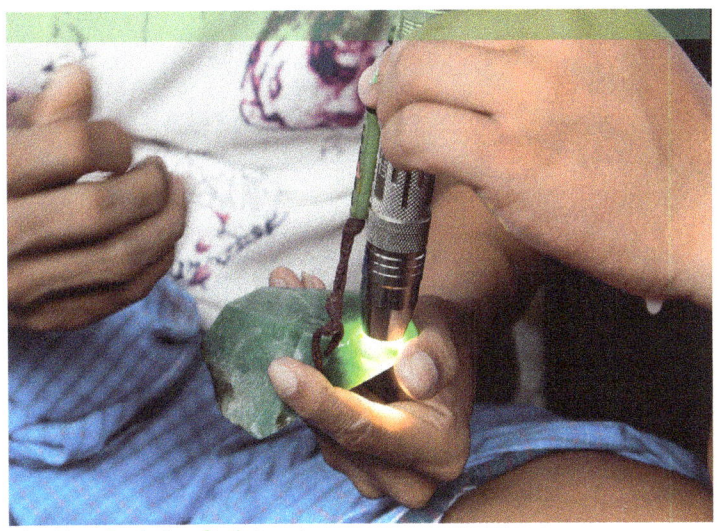

Checking the clarity of jade to cut © Kim Rix

Cut

The very highest quality jadeite is usually reserved only for beads or cabochons. A well-cut cabochon should be well proportioned, smoothly curved and have a dome that is not too high or too flat. A string of beads should be as uniform as possible in colour, texture and translucency. Good quality jadeite, as well as being used for cabochons and beads, is often cut into a flattened doughnut shape called a 'pi' and worn on a thread as a necklace. You'll also see it cut into bangles, rings and small figurines, some of which are beautifully carved. Bangles and rings that have been cut from a single piece of stone are called 'hololiths', and cost a great deal more than those formed from different pieces of jade joined together.

A very fine jade necklace © Kim Rix

Classes of jade

You will probably come across the descriptor 'Imperial jade'. Rough Burmese jade is categorised into one of three classes: **imperial**, **commercial** or **utility**.

Imperial jade is extremely high quality and describes jade that is a uniform, emerald green and translucent to semi-transparent. It is used in the very finest jewellery. It is called Imperial jade because the Chinese character for 'jade' looks very similar to the character for 'emperor'. It was also the case that the very finest specimens were once reserved for the Chinese royal court.

Commercial jade describes stones that are creamy in colour, a less vivid and uniform shade of green or less transparent than imperial jade. Purple jade is sometimes included in this category. Commercial jade is used in jewellery and also for statues and carvings.

Utility jade is usually white, brown or black, though more desirable shades may find their way into this class if they are flawed, dull or opaque. You will find utility jade sold as decorations, knick-knacks, keychains and cheap jewellery.

Treatment of jade

As well as the classes of jade mentioned previously, jade is classified according to the form of treatment it has undergone.

Type A

Type A is the classification given to natural jade that has undergone only the traditional, superficial treatments of washing and waxing. The polished piece of jade is washed in a mildly acidic bath (traditionally plum vinegar) to remove any leftover debris from the polishing process. It is then polished with paraffin wax (traditionally beeswax) to enhance its natural sheen. Washing and waxing does not affect the structure or integrity of the jade.

Type B
Type B jade has undergone a process of chemical bleaching and filling. The jade is first bleached to remove undesirable inclusions. Traditionally, this was done by submersing the jade in an acidic plum vinegar bath for several hours and then soaking it in warm wax to fill any fissures and holes, giving the jade a smooth, glossy surface. Nowadays, modern bleaches and polymers are used. Unlike the gentle acid wash given to Type A jade, the bleach treatment given to Type B jade affects the structural integrity of the stone, making it more brittle. Over time, heat and exposure to household chemicals will cause the polymer filling and coating to degrade and discolour.

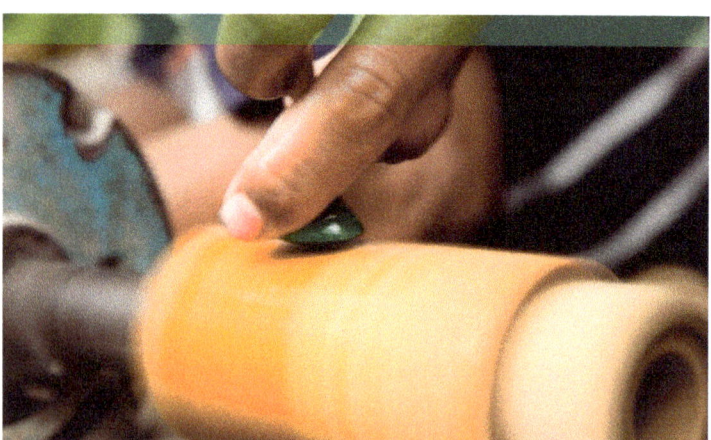

Shaping and polishing the jade © Kim Rix

BUYING GEMSTONES IN MYANMAR

At the jade market, Mandalay © Kim Rix

Type C

Type C jade refers to jade that has been dyed. Dying is the most common form of jadeite treatment and is usually used to give white (or bleached) jade the more desirable colours of green or lavender. Dyed jade is subject to discolouration, as heat and sunlight cause the dyes to break down.

The quality of the original jade determines how easy it is to detect whether your piece of jade has been dyed. Remember my paragraph on the texture of jade? The texture of a piece of jade depends on how closely its crystal granules are interlocked. Very broadly speaking, jade with a coarse texture has large, irregular and loosely interlocked granules, whereas fine-textured jade has granules that are small, regular and tightly packed together. Dye pools unevenly in the coarse jade and so is easier to spot, especially if you use a 10X jeweller's loupe. It's much harder to tell with fine textured jade as the small granules take the dye very well. Always have your gem tested!

About Burmese ruby

90% of the world's high-end rubies are mined in Myanmar. Many people think of diamond, the hardest gemstone, as the king of jewels. But in Myanmar, ruby is king and rubies mined here are the standard by which all rubies are judged.

Ruby is a variety of a mineral called corundum, the same mineral as sapphire. The two gemstones are distinguished by colour alone, as their structure is the same. Red corundum is called ruby, whereas corundum of any other colour is called sapphire. It's the inclusion of different elements within the structure that causes the variations in colour – in a ruby, trace elements of chromium turn the corundum red. Corundum measures 9 on the Mohs scale, which makes ruby a very tough stone and an excellent choice for setting within a frequently worn ring.

There are three ruby-producing regions in Myanmar of importance. Mogok, Mong Hsu (pronounced 'Mong Shu') and Namya or Namya Seik. Known as **The Burmese Ruby Triangle**, these produce high quality rubies.

A fourth region, Pyin Lon in the Northern Shan state, produces only low quality rubies.

A region lying 200km north of Mandalay, the mines of Mogok are legendary for producing the world's finest rubies. These highly sought-after Burmese rubies are prized primarily for their colour, referred to as *Ko-thwe* (pigeon blood). The term 'pigeon blood' describes a particularly vibrant, pure red with a purplish tint. A lab certificate that states the colour is pigeon blood will add value to a ruby.

Burmese Ruby Necklace, Fine Gems & Jewellery, Yangon © Kim Rix

Mong Hsu is a region in the southern Shan state. Mong Hsu rubies are the same colour as some spinel so they could easily be confused. Mong Hsu rubies are almost always darker than Mogok rubies and need to be heat treated.

The Namya mines are situated in Kachin State, northern Myanmar, east of the Hpa Kant Jade mine.

You will see 'pigeon blood' and 'Burmese' used interchangeably to refer to Burmese rubies. It is important to note that there is no universal standard to define what counts as a pigeon blood ruby. Different labs have different criteria, with some using origin and others using colour as a guide.

Because of this, not all Burmese rubies are regarded as pigeon blood rubies. Conversely, the description 'pigeon blood' does not necessarily mean that a ruby is Burmese – Mozambique, for example, has produced rubies that some labs have identified as pigeon blood. However, if you were to put two rubies of equal quality and size on the market, the Burmese ruby would almost certainly attract a much higher price thanks to the fame and desirability of its origin.

The best-known Burmese rubies include an 8-carat ruby that was fashioned into a ring by Van Cleef & Arpels and given as a Christmas gift to Elizabeth Taylor by Richard Burton in 1968, who told her that he had waited for the most perfect ruby in the world. The ring achieved $4.22 million at Christie's in 2011. Elizabeth Taylor was also given a Cartier Burmese ruby and diamond suite by her third husband, Mike Todd, which is worth over $5 million. Another remarkable ruby is the Carmen Lucia Ruby. It weighs 23.1 carats and is one of the largest faceted rubies in the world.

Caring for rubies: Ultrasonic and steam cleaners are usually safe for untreated and heat-treated stones. Fracture-filled, cavity-filled, or dyed material should only be cleaned with a damp cloth. Warm, soapy water is always the safest option.

About Burmese sapphire

Burmese sapphire © Kim Rix

Like Burmese ruby, Burmese sapphire is considered exceptionally high quality. Though rubies are mined in greater quantity in Myanmar, the sapphires produced by the mines in Mogok tend to be bigger.

Burmese sapphire is second only to that from Kashmir in terms of its desirability, though – as with ruby – origin has become somewhat of a 'designer label.' A sapphire mined in Myanmar will cost at least 50-100% (and sometimes much more) than an equivalent sapphire mined elsewhere.

The intense, almost violet, blue of the best Burmese sapphires is down to the presence of iron and titanium and was once considered 'too dark' by some in the gemstone trade. In fact Burmese sapphires range in colour from a deep royal blue to a lighter cornflower blue and most dealers now consider the stronger saturation of the best Burmese sapphires highly desirable.

As well as blue sapphire, star sapphire is also found in Myanmar, with the mine at Kabaing, in Mogok, particularly famous for this. Star sapphire is one of the 'phenomenal' gemstones – that is, gemstones that display interesting optical effects. In the case of star sapphires, dense, linear inclusions of titanium dioxide known as 'rutile' (or 'silk') reflect light in such a way that a star appears to float across the surface of the stone. This is known as **asterism**. Depending on the nature of the rutile, this star can have four, six or twelve rays.

The main thing that you need to keep in mind when buying sapphire is that there are many gemstones that look like sapphire but aren't. These include blue spinel, iolite (often sold as 'water sapphire') and kyanite, among others. Always do your homework!

On the other hand, white, orange, yellow or brown sapphire sometimes (confusingly) goes by the name King Topaz. Sapphire is expensive, so you'd be doing well to get it for the price of a topaz!

Caring for sapphires: Care for sapphires in the same way as you would rubies. Ultrasonic and steam cleaners are usually safe for untreated, heat-treated, and lattice diffusion treated stones. Fracture-filled, cavity-filled, or dyed material should only be cleaned with a damp cloth. To be safe, warm, soapy water is always best.

BUYING GEMSTONES IN MYANMAR

Ruby and sapphire: knowing what you're looking at

A good knowledge base is essential when buying your Burmese ruby or sapphire. Whatever your price point, you'll want to avoid paying more than your gem is worth.

Gemstones are generally categorised using the Four Cs: colour, clarity, cut and carat. With rubies and sapphires, you'll also need to consider origin and treatment.

Colour

Colour is the most important factor in the price of a ruby or sapphire. It's not as simple as a gemstone being 'blue' or 'red', though. A gemstone's colour actually incorporates three separate aspects: the saturation, the hue, and the tone.

Burmese ruby © Kim Rix

Gemstone carvings © Kim Rix

Saturation

Saturation refers to the amount of colour in the stone. A stone's saturation is the most important factor in its valuation. Stones with low saturation may appear washed out, whereas stones with high saturation may appear too dark. The most valuable stones have medium saturation. Burmese sapphires were once considered to have too high a saturation, but many are now prized for their intensity.

Hue

Hue is a more specific term for colour and refers to the particular shade of the stone's colour. Rubies are described by their primary (dominant) and secondary hue. To be classed as a ruby, the primary hue must be red; if it's any other colour, the stone is considered a sapphire. In a written description of any gemstone, the primary hue will have a capital letter and the secondary hue will have a lower case letter. For example, you might see a ruby described as 'Red' or 'Red-orange' and a sapphire described as 'greenish Blue', 'Orange-pink', or simply 'Blue'. The best quality sapphires have only one hue, and blue is the most prized. The most expensive rubies are a pure red to red with a hint of blue, or 'pigeon blood' – this is the colour for which Mogok's mines are so famous. Rubies at the Red-orange end of the spectrum are generally less expensive.

Tone
The tone refers to the depth of colour in a stone – how light or dark it appears. A stone that is too light won't show the colour to its best effect, whereas a stone that is too dark will lack brilliance. Make sure that you look at your stone in both artificial and natural light. Cup your hand over it. The stone should appear lively and brilliant, even in shade.

Setting your ruby in yellow or rose gold will best accentuate its colour and brilliance. A blue sapphire looks best against white gold, platinum or silver. However, you should go for what you feel suits your skin tone and personal taste.

Clarity
Rubies and sapphires usually have **inclusions** (flaws) when seen under a microscope, so if you are shown a stone that looks flawless under magnification, ask yourself, "Is it too good to be true?" However, the inclusions in a high-quality stone shouldn't be visible to the naked eye. The position of inclusions also affects the price. A stone with inclusions in the centre will generally be cheaper than an equivalent stone with an inclusion nearer the edge, for obvious aesthetic reasons.

Cut

The quality and type of cut affects the value. When cutting a gemstone, the aim is to retain as much of the weight as possible while achieving the most beautiful effect. It's a fine balancing act! Round and oval cuts are common for rubies, whereas sapphire is often found cut as an oval or cushion. That's because these cuts enhance each stone's **lustre** while keeping its weight as high as possible. They're also stylish and easy to set in a piece of jewellery. Watch out for areas that don't reflect light and so don't seem to sparkle. These are called **windows** and they detract from the brilliance and value of the stone. A gem with a large face and a shallow bottom will produce this effect.

To check for windowing, place the gem on a piece of paper with text on it and look directly down on it at an angle of 90%. If there is a lighter area in the middle through which you can read the text, the gem has a window.

Most stones will demonstrate windowing to some degree when viewed at an angle. What you need to watch out for is windowing that is obvious when viewed directly from above.

Carat

Carats are units of weight in gemstone terminology. The higher the carat, the heavier and more expensive the gemstone. Price per carat increases at 2, 3 and 4 carats. A 4-carat stone will cost more per carat than a 2-carat stone because of the rarity of larger stones.

Top Tip: it is rare to find stones over 5 carats, so beware if you are shown a large ruby or sapphire at what seems like a surprisingly low price.

Origin

As discussed in the previous chapter, Myanmar is the most highly rated location in the world for ruby and the second most highly rated for sapphire. A gemstone's origin can often function like a designer label! The most prized sapphires come from Kashmir and Myanmar, followed by Sri Lanka and Madagascar.

Star ruby and sapphire

Along with a handful of other gemstones, ruby and sapphires sometimes display a four, six or twelve rayed star that appears to float beneath the surface of the gem. This optical effect is called **asterism** and is caused by light reflecting off needle-like flaws orientated along the faces of the crystal structure. Star gemstones are cut and polished in a smooth-domed cabochon, as this cut displays the asterism to its best effect. They are priced according to the intensity and attractiveness of the body colour and the strength and sharpness of the star. It is rare to find a star ruby or sapphire in which both colour and star are equally fine.

Burmese star ruby © Kim Rix

Spotting a fake: a synthetic star ruby will often look 'too perfect', with rays that are straight and/or of equal length. If the star doesn't appear to move when the stone is turned, the star ruby is certainly not natural. However, synthetic star rubies can have moving stars – get yours checked at a lab.

 Top Tip: a red star ruby is much rarer than a white star ruby

Treatment of ruby and sapphire

95% of all gemstones sold worldwide have been treated in some way. With rubies and sapphires, the figure is closer to 99%. Treatment is the norm and something that you shouldn't usually worry about – unless you are intending to buy a natural, unheated gemstone, in which case you would be investing thousands of pounds and would expect it to come with a lab report. Be on your guard if someone tries to sell you a good-looking, 'untreated' stone!

In Myanmar, the treatment of gemstones is uncommon. What you need to know is that most of the gemstones from Mogok are not treated but Mong Hsu rubies are almost always treated.

 Top Tip: be aware that most of the rubies you will see at Bogyoke Aung San Market in Yangon will be glass filled and heat treated. These rubies are mostly from Africa, not Myanmar.

Before you buy any gemstone, you should always check its certificate or get it tested for authenticity. You'll find details of how to do this later in the chapter.

Other gemstones found in Myanmar

Though Myanmar is best known for its jadeite, ruby and sapphire, you may well be tempted by the other beautiful gemstones on offer! Myanmar has produced many other interesting gemstones, including aquamarine, zircon, amethyst, peridot, pearl, topaz, tourmaline, lapis lazuli, spinel and amber.

This chapter gives you a brief guide to the other gems you're most likely to see for sale, mined in Myanmar.

Agate *(kone pale)*

Agate is a translucent, banded form of chalcedony and silica that comes in a wide range of colours. The colours occur in bands caused by differing impurities as the layers formed within the stone. The best quality agate is used in jewellery.

Caring for agate: Wash with warm, soapy water.

How to spot fake agate: Glass 'agate' may contain bubbles and obvious swirls of colour rather than bands. It's hard to imitate the natural banding of agate. Very brightly coloured agate is probably dyed.

Amber *(pa yin)*

Amber is the fossilized resin of long-extinct trees and occurs in different colours, the most common being yellow or orange, followed by green. Rarer colours include red and blue. Burmese amber, considered some of the highest quality amber in the world, is found in the Hukawng Valley in Northern Myanmar. Less

expensive than jade, amber is also believed to be good for your health. It is said to be especially helpful for restful sleep, which is why you will see amber pillows on sale, stuffed with ground-up pieces of discarded amber. Myitkyina and the Ta Naing area hold open-air amber markets, but please be aware that civil unrest is still a possibility here. If you have your heart set on buying amber in Myanmar, buy from Mandalay, Yangon or Mogok.

Caring for amber: wash in warm, soapy water.

How to spot a fake amber: Plastic amber will melt if heated. However, I don't advise you try this! A better test is to sniff the amber – warm it in your hands first. If it smells of pine tree resin, it's probably genuine.

Amethyst *(kayan swal)*
Amethyst is a purple variety of quartz. It was once considered a precious gem, but was downgraded to semi-precious status after large reserves of it were uncovered in Brazil. Burmese amethyst is noted for its quality and deep purple colour.

Caring for amethyst: wash in warm, soapy water

How to spot fake amethyst: Real amethyst feels cool to the touch and takes a few seconds to warm up when placed on the skin. Glass warms quickly and may contain bubbles or streaks/patches of dye.

Aquamarine *(salin seinn)*
Aquamarine is a blue to blueish-green variety of the mineral beryl. Its colour is due to trace amounts of iron within the mineral structure, and stones are often heat treated to remove the greenish hues. In

Myanmar, aquamarine is found in the Sakangyi area in the west of the Mogok stone tract, but the majority of the world's aquamarine is mined in Brazil.

Caring for aquamarine: wash in warm, soapy water

How to spot a fake: the simplest way to determine whether an aquamarine is real, or simply coloured glass, is to look carefully at your stone. If you see scratches on the surface, it is most likely a fake.

Chrysoberyl

Rather confusingly, chrysoberyl is not a beryl at all. It is from a different family of the mineral beryl and is a relative of the gemstone alexandrite. Unlike alexandrite, however, chrysoberyl does not appear to change colour in different lighting conditions. Chrysoberyl is usually yellow to yellowish-green in colour, with stones at the greener end of the spectrum the most prized.

Cat's eye chrysoberyl *(kyaung myat lone)*

Because it exhibits an exceptionally strong and well-defined line, cat's eye chrysoberyl is considered the finest example of **chatoyancy**. If you illuminate cat's eye chrysoberyl from the side, it will appear to be milky white on one side of the line and its natural colour on the other.

Caring for chrysoberyl and Cat's eye chrysoberyl: as a fairly hardy gemstone at 8.5 on the Mohs scale, ultrasonic and steam cleaning should be safe for both.

How to spot a fake: Firstly, real cat's eye chrysoberyl is rare, exotic and expensive. Secondly, in nature, a real cat's eye chrysoberyl might not be perfectly formed or brightly coloured. Imitation cat's eyes are made from coloured glass and if the stripe of the eye looks too sharp and perfect, question whether it is real. A natural cat's eye will display in all kinds of light, especially in the dark!

Coral *(thandar)*

Like the bones in our body and pearls, coral is made of calcium carbonate. It's formed from the skeleton-like structures of underwater organisms called coral polyps, which are harvested and polished to produce beads, cabochons and irregular-shaped branches for use in jewellery. Red, or 'precious,' coral is deep red to pink in colour, and was traditionally harvested in the Mediterranean, though coral decimation in this part of the world means that precious coral is now harvested elsewhere.

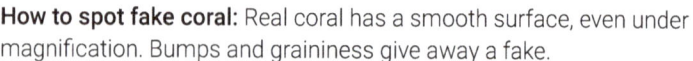

Caring for coral: Coral is very soft and should never be put in an ultrasonic cleaner or jewellery cleaning solution. Use warm, soapy water only.

How to spot fake coral: Real coral has a smooth surface, even under magnification. Bumps and graininess give away a fake.

Garnet *(u daung)*

'Garnet' is an umbrella term for a group of closely-related varieties of mineral. It occurs in a range of colours, but beautiful Myanmar garnets are orange and purple-red. Warm reddish hessonite is the most commonly occurring garnet, and the orange-coloured spessartite the most expensive.

Caring for garnet: Do not steam clean garnets. You may put your garnet in an ultrasonic cleaner, except for demantoid garnet. If in doubt, clean your garnet with warm, soapy water and a soft brush.

How to spot a fake: The easiest method is to look at the garnet in both natural and artificial light. Take it outdoors, then bring it indoors. Does the colour look slightly different in each light? A real garnet should look a slightly different colour in natural light. Or, look through the stone: if you see lots of inclusions, your stone is probably not a garnet. This is because garnets generally have good clarity.

Iolite

Iolite has been known to be called 'water sapphire' because its colour can be very similar to genuine blue sapphire. Be aware that the two are very different gemstones! Derived from the Greek word 'ios', meaning 'violet', iolite occurs in shades of purple, blue and grey. Iolite is becoming popular as an affordable alternative to more expensive stones like sapphire and tanzanite. Though reasonably durable, it is still softer than tough sapphire and so should be treated with a little care. No treatment has yet been used successfully on iolite, so you can assume that any particularly fine example will be entirely natural.

Caring for your iolite: Iolite should not be cleaned with heat steamers or ultrasonic cleaners. To clean your iolite, simply use warm, soapy water and a soft cloth.

How to spot a fake: iolite is easily confused with tanzanite and sapphire, but iolite 'fakes' will generally be coloured glass. As glass is much softer than Iolite, it may be scratched – a good clue!

Lapis Lazuli

High quality lapis lazuli is a metamorphic rock prized for its deep blue colour. The golden specks that appear in many specimens are pyrite. It makes a good gemstone for bold pieces of jewellery, as it's often found in very large chunks.

Caring for lapis lazuli: Wash in warm, soapy water.

How to spot a fake: Fake lapis lazuli lacks the intensity and depth of blue in a real stone and will often appear flat and more opaque.

Moonstone *(myaw kyauk)*

Moonstone is an exquisite semi-precious gemstone that appears to flash and glow from within, thanks to an optical effect called **adularescence**. Varieties of moonstone are found across the globe, and blue moonstone (found only in Sri Lanka) is more expensive than other types, due to its rarity.

Moonstone is traditionally cut in the form of a cabochon – a smooth, unfaceted round, oval or teardrop shape.

Caring for moonstone: Moonstone is not very tough, so will need careful handling. It's probably not an ideal gemstone for everyday jewellery likely to get knocked. Wash with warm, soapy water.

How to spot a fake: Opalite is a man-made glass stone often sold as 'moonstone'. Real moonstone tends to have visible layers, cracks and inclusions within the stone, and seems to flash when the stone is turned. Opalite is perfectly clear and its glow is softer and more even.

Pearl *(palel)*

Burmese pearls are cultivated in the clean waters of the Myeik Archipelago, 400 miles south of Yangon, and are famous in the world jewellery market. The most coveted of these South Sea pearls are a variety called 'Melo', which are formed in a type of very large sea snail rather than in oysters or clams. Melo pearls are orange with pinkish tones and, unlike other pearls, are not composed of layers of nacre but of calcite and aragonite.

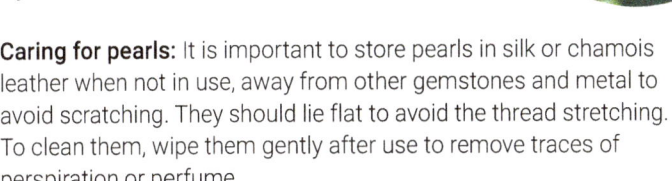

Caring for pearls: It is important to store pearls in silk or chamois leather when not in use, away from other gemstones and metal to avoid scratching. They should lie flat to avoid the thread stretching. To clean them, wipe them gently after use to remove traces of perspiration or perfume.

How to spot a fake: generally speaking, the surface of an authentic natural pearl is gritty and unevenly shaped. It will also feel cold to the touch. Imitation pearls, on the other hand, will feel warm, look beautifully smooth and be perfectly rounded. Look around the hole to detect chipped paint, and through the hole to detect glass or plastic.

Peridot *(pyaung guang seinn)*

Peridot, a variety of the mineral olivine, is mined at Pyaung Gaung in Mogok. An **idiochromatic** gem, peridot occurs in only one colour: green. However, its precise hue depends on the amount of iron present in the crystal structure and can range from a bright, citrusy shade to a deeper, grassier colour. It is this deeper and more intense hue that is considered the most desirable.

The Pyaung Gaung mines in Mogok have also produced star-peridot, enstatite and chrysoprase.

Caring for peridot: do not clean your peridot in an ultrasonic or steam cleaner – these could damage your gemstone. It is best to clean them with soap and warm water.

How to spot a fake: you can do a quick test just by looking at peridot. True Peridot is green. Take it outside: if the colour doesn't change between daylight and artificial light, that's a good sign. Now look for a yellow or brown tint. Even the best quality peridot has a slight yellow tint.

Sphene

Sphene, or titanite, is a gemstone that occurs in shades of lime green to orangey brown, depending on the level of iron present in the stone. It's prized for its spectacular fire, which is more intense even than that of diamond. The name 'sphene' comes from the Greek word for 'wedge' and refers to the shape of its crystals. Large sphene gemstones are hardly ever found, so it's rare to see one of more than about 1 or 2 carats on sale.

Caring for sphene: Sphene is one of the softest gemstones suitable for use in jewellery, so should not be set in a ring. The best way to clean sphene is with warm, soapy water. Never use an ultrasonic cleaner or steamer.

How to spot a fake: Real sphene is expensive. It will almost always have inclusions and is very rarely 'eye clean'.

Spinel *(a nyant)*

Of all the gemstones in Myanmar, you'll probably see more spinel than anything else. You might have to hunt for one with good clarity, but you'll see a myriad of colours along the way. In general, red spinel is the most desirable – and therefore valuable – followed by fine, rare, cobalt-blue spinel.

Myanmar is known for the high quality of its spinel, which is found in Mogok and more recently in Kachin Province, east of the area where jadeite is mined.

Burmese spinel has often been mistaken for ruby in the past, thanks to its hue and strong **fluorescence** (the ability to absorb ultraviolet light and emit it as visible light). Probably the best example is the 170 carat cabochon known as 'The Black Prince's Ruby', which sits in the British imperial state crown but was later determined to be a spinel after mineralogist Louis Rom de Lisle identified spinel as a separate mineral from ruby in 1783.

Caring for spinel: keep spinel away from heat to avoid the colour fading and wash with soapy water.

How to spot a fake: It's difficult to distinguish natural spinel from lab-grown, synthetic spinel. If you carry a loupe, you might see gas bubbles in a synthetic. If in doubt, take it to a professional to get it properly assessed.

 Top Tip: green is the rarest colour of spinel and is one of the most likely to be synthetic.

Topaz *(oattha paya)*

Topaz, widely found in Myanmar, occurs as a colourless stone as well as in shades of pink, purple, yellow, brown, orange, green and blue. Topaz is **allochromatic**, i.e. the colour variations are caused by impurities or defects in its chemical structure. It's also **pleochroic**, which means that it will display different colours when its crystal structure is observed from different angles.

Caring for topaz: Topaz is a hard gemstone on the Mohs scale but will chip or crack if given a hard knock. Some topaz (like mystic topaz) is coated. That coating can be easily scratched, so topaz should generally be handled with care. It is best to clean topaz in warm, soapy water and rub gently with a cloth.

How to spot a fake: cheap quartz is sometimes used in place of topaz. A real topaz is cool to touch and can be electrostatically charged easily. To test, rub topaz against a woollen cloth then hover the stone over your hair.

Tourmaline *(paye u)*

If you're a mineral collector, look out for tourmaline in Myanmar where various colours and different forms of tourmaline can be found: rough, cut, cabochon and crystal.

Caring for tourmaline: Warm, soapy water is the best method for cleaning tourmaline.

How to spot a fake: Gas bubbles indicate glass. If there are no inclusions, the gemstone could be synthetic. Look at your stone from every direction – there should be a slight change in colour depending on the viewing angle. That's because tourmaline is pleochroic.

Zircon *(gaw mate)*

Zircon is widely found in Myanmar. Zircon occurs in a range of colours, of which blue is the most valuable. Colourless zircon can be a cheaper alternative to diamond, due to its excellent lustre and brilliance. Don't confuse the semi-precious gemstone zircon with a synthetic imitation diamond called cubic zirconia, though – they are two separate substances! Zircon is softer than diamond, so take care wearing zircon jewellery every day. It also tends to darken and grow dull when exposed to regular sunlight.

Caring for zircon: ultrasonic and steam cleaners are not recommended for cleaning zircon. Clean by hand in warm, soapy water and gently rub with a cloth.

How to spot a fake: Zircon is the world's oldest natural gemstone and is a cheap gemstone to buy, except possibly for green zircon, the rarest colour of all zircon. There are many imitations and white zircon is a go-to diamond substitute. If you are buying a diamond, make sure you get a lab report.

A set of blue zircon © *Kim Rix*

Birthstones by month:

Month		Stone
January		Garnet
February		Amethyst
March		Aquamarine
April		Diamond
May		Emerald
June		Alexandrite or pearl
July		Ruby
August		Peridot
September		Sapphire
October		Tourmaline or opal
November		Topaz or citrine
December		Turquoise, tanzanite or Zircon

The Navaratna

On your visit to Myanmar, you will almost certainly come across the term 'Navaratna' – a Sanskrit word meaning 'nine gems.' Referred to as Naoratna in Burmese, Navaratna is a piece of jewellery set with a combination of nine gemstones, which ancient astrology connects with nine astronomical bodies.

Though the origins of Navaratna jewellery are uncertain, the association of gemstones with the stars, moons and planets is found in ancient Hindu texts. The Navaratna has cultural significance across India and south-east Asia, where its gems are believed to harness the positive characteristics and ward off the negative energies of the nine major celestial bodies in Hindu astrology. Belief in the power of the Navaratna is common to many religions, including Hinduism, Buddhism, Jainism and Sikhism.

Astrologists believe that the position of the stars and planets at our birth affects the course of our life. Because of this, the arrangement of the gemstones in each piece of Navaratna jewellery is significant. Ruby, which represents the sun, tends to be found at the centre of the arrangement. Many people who wear the Navaratna will consult an astrologer before having the stones set in an arrangement that is considered particularly lucky for them.

Traditionally, gems used in the Navaratna should have good clarity. Gemstones that are cracked or significantly flawed are thought to block the passage of light through the gemstones and so weaken – or even reverse – their desired effects.

The nine gems and the planets associated with them are as follows:

Gem	Planet		Characteristics
Ruby		The sun	Power and success
Pearl		The moon	Spirit and emotion
Coral		Mars	Strength and courage
Diamond		Venus	Beauty and harmony
Yellow sapphire		Jupiter	Knowledge
Blue sapphire		Saturn	Prosperity, good health and fame
Emerald		Mercury	Intelligence, communication and humour
Hessonite garnet	Rahu*		fearlessness, clarity and spiritual growth
Cat's eye chrysoberyl	Ketu*		Liberation, enlightenment and spirituality

* Rahu and Ketu are spirits or demons who appear in Hindu, Buddhist and Jain texts. Rahu embodies the solar eclipse and Ketu the lunar (or, in astronomical terms, the ascending and descending lunar nodes).

Did you know?
- 9 gems simply means 9 gems – diamonds are not compulsory!
- Coral comes in 5 or 6 colours. Only orange coral is used in Navratna jewels.
- If you are bad mannered whilst wearing the Navaratna, it is said to attract bad vibes back at you.
- It is likely that the emerald in Navaratna jewellery comes from India or Colombia.

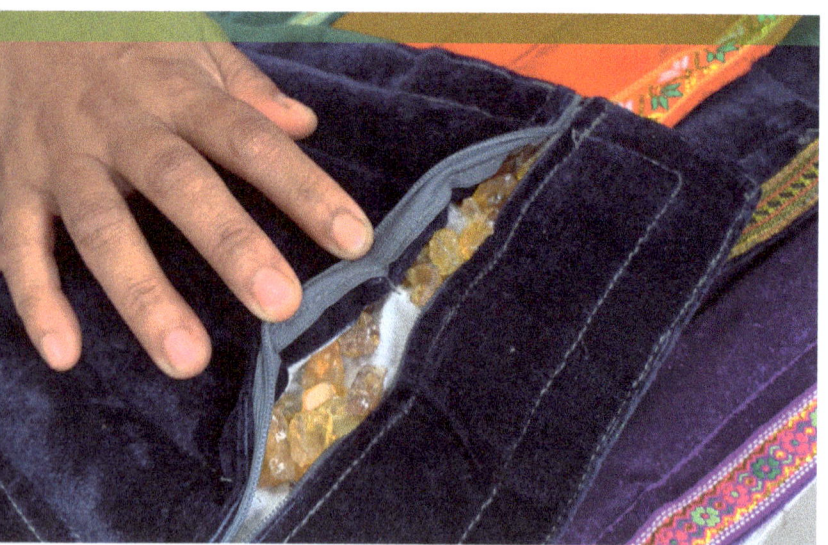

Amber pillows to aid sleep © Kim Rix

Spotting a fake

There are four categories of gemstone you need to be aware of:

- Natural and unheated/untreated

- Natural, yet heated/treated

- Synthetic (the gemstone has the same physical and chemical properties as a natural stone, but was created in a laboratory rather than in the earth)

- Imitation or simulants (a cheaper material made to look like a valuable gemstone) created in a laboratory

The gemstone information in the **'Knowing what you're looking at'** sections will give you a good head start, but you need to keep in mind that even experts can't always make an accurate identification with the naked eye.

You can – and should – have your gemstone tested before you hand over any money, even if it already has a certificate of authenticity or 'written guarantee'. This is simply a piece of paper confirming that your gemstone is real, according to the seller. However, anyone can write a certificate!

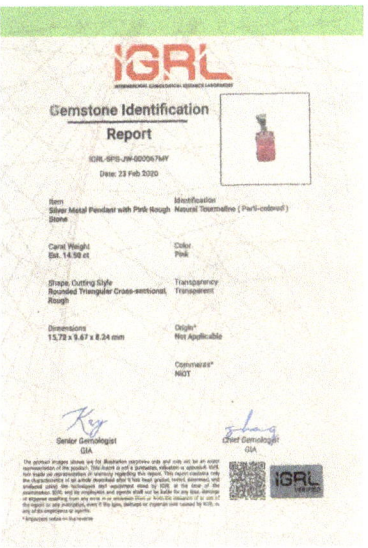

A laboratory identification report goes into more detail about the stone. If you do want to get a proper report for your gemstone, you can visit one of the reputable gem labs in Myanmar.

Top Tips – How to spot a fake jade?

- Real jade has a high density, whereas imitation jade (often glass or plastic) will feel light in your hand.
- Imitation jade may contain air bubbles when you shine a light through it and will make a clanking or clicking sound, like that of marbles or plastic beads when you tap two pieces together. Real jade makes a higher pitched, almost chiming, noise when you do this.
- Genuine jade will feel cool to the touch and will take a few moments to warm up in your hand, whereas glass or plastic will rapidly acquire your body temperature.

Gemstone simulants

A simulant or imitation is a cheap gemstone that looks like a more precious one. These are a few to look out for in Myanmar:

- Skolarite looks like lapis lazuli, though without the gold flecks of pyrite
- Mogok chrome diopside looks just like emerald
- Garnet could be confused with red spinel or ruby
- Kyanite can appear similar to blue sapphire
- Danburite looks like white sapphire but is ever so slightly brighter

BUYING GEMSTONES IN MYANMAR

Buying in Myanmar: three things you need to know

1. Myanmar is an expensive place to buy

You should keep in mind that it will be more expensive buying gemstones in Myanmar than buying them in Thailand or Sri Lanka, for example. Burmese gemstones are some of the finest in the world, especially jade, ruby and sapphire. The descriptor 'Burmese' before a gemstone can increase the price ten times, and sometimes much, much more.

2. Gem sales are regulated

In Myanmar, gemstone traders must apply to the state-owned Myanmar Gems Enterprise (MGE) for a government licence. They are issued with an official cash memo book to record purchases. Note that there is a $50,000 limit on individual sales – for sales above this value, the vendor is required to notify the regulatory bodies and to make the sale at a location specified by the Ministry of Mines.

The majority of smaller shops will display a sign saying "Government Licensed"; big brands don't tend to bother, as they are already known in the local market and their compliance with the regulations is understood.

Of course, as in every country, there are people trading under the radar or finding ways to work around the rules!

3. Be ready to declare your purchases

You will need the MGE cash memo book receipt for your gems when you leave Myanmar, as travellers – including tourists – are expected to declare any gems or jewellery they have bought while in the country. You will be given two receipts: the original receipt and a carbon copy to give to customs, thus proving that you have bought from a licensed seller who has paid the government tax. Be aware that any certification or gemmological paperwork you receive should be in addition to these receipts.

IMPORTANT: You will need your passport number to complete the MGE receipt. If you don't want to carry your passport around with you, make sure you have jotted down the number to keep in your wallet.

With these three points in mind, if you are keen to come back with a memento of your trip, or are attached to the idea of owning a Burmese gemstone that you've actually bought in the country of its origin, then here are some options to consider.

Natural, polished cabochon gemstones © Kim Rix

BUYING GEMSTONES IN MYANMAR

Deciding what you want

There are a few questions you need to ask yourself before purchasing:

Loose stone or set?
If you can't find a piece of ready-made jewellery that suits your taste, why not buy a loose gemstone? There are many jewellers in Myanmar who will be able to set your stone in jewellery for you, or you can take it home for your preferred jeweller to do the job.

What's the stone for?
Are you intending to set your gemstone in a ring, a brooch, a bracelet, a necklace? Think about how the size and cut of your gemstone will affect the look of the piece. Whether buying a loose gemstone or a finished piece, make sure you consider the toughness of the gemstone. A soft gemstone in an everyday ring won't last long.

How much do I want to spend?
This is important. You need to decide on a budget before you approach anywhere that sells gemstones. It's easy to get carried away and spend more than you can really afford, particularly in an unfamiliar currency.

At the Tray market © Kim Rix

A large specimen of aquamarine rough © Kim Rix

How do I want to pay?
How you want to pay will affect where you buy. For making significant purchases in Mandalay and Yangon, you can use a credit card but it's unlikely you'll be able to pay with plastic in Mogok and you'll certainly need to pay in cash at any market. Take plenty of US dollars (in new condition) and change where necessary.

Where do I want to do my gemstone shopping?
Knowing your budget and how you want to pay should determine where you should buy: a luxury hotel, a large and established jewellery shop, at a jewellery show, in a museum, at a small gemstone merchant/trader or at the gemstone market. Let's look at those options more closely...

Choosing where to buy

Option 1: buying from a shop
It's more advisable for a tourist who is inexperienced in gemstones to buy from a shop, even though you'll pay more in a shop than in the market. If there is any issue with a shop-bought gemstone, you can more easily go back to the place to complain.

For a gemstone or piece of jewellery, think about the kind of establishment you are in. A shop or dealer with a reputation to uphold will have a real and serious interest in selling you genuine goods.

Famous brands in Myanmar include: Manaw May Ya, She Shine, Elegant Gems, Golden Palace (famous for gold and jewellery) and Htay Paing (famous for rubies).

Option 2: buying from a gemstone merchant/dealer
Buying through a merchant will probably be cheaper than buying in a shop, but it is not as straightforward for the inexperienced tourist.

If you already have contacts in Myanmar, ask them for a recommendation. Remember that a gem merchant who appears in this book will have a reputation to uphold. Their livelihood depends on their reputation, whereas an unregistered tourist guide or taxi driver has less to lose.

Option 3: buying from an outdoor street market
Buying at a market can be a little intimidating for a newbie, but it's a lot of fun. The Mandalay jade market is a destination in itself – and an absolute maze!

If this is what you want to do, then I strongly recommend that you don't go without a guide. Do be aware that not all brokers are licensed

– anybody can become one. However, it's a word of mouth industry. If a broker behaves dishonestly, everyone gets to know and the broker will go out of business.

 Top Tip: cash is king in Myanmar, especially at the gem market

You'll get a feel for the hustle and bustle of the gem trade from an outdoor market, but be aware that they are crowded and chaotic.

Turn to the chapters on Yangon, Mandalay and Mogok for information on the individual gemstone markets there.

Option 4: buying at a jewellery show

Myanmar hosts a handful of gem and jewellery shows.

The authorities of the Myanmar Gems and Jewellery Entrepreneurs Association (MGJEA) look after six regional associations – Yangon, Mandalay, Sagaing, Myit Kyi Na, Hpa Kant and Mogok – and organise gem shows in Yangon, Mandalay, Sagaing and Myit Ki Na. The MGJEA first show, The International Gems and Jewellery Show in 2018, was such a success that it became an annual event.

Myanmar Gems and Jewellery Entrepreneurs Association (MGJEA)

Contact: Dr Aung Kyaw Win, Vice Chairman
Tel: +95 9 426219597
Tel: +95 9 788892682
Web: www.mgjea.org

Option 5: buying from a gem museum

Gem museums in Myanmar tend to be add-ons to the real business of trading gems. For example, the Myanmar Gems Museum occupies the top floor of a building that also houses the government-run Gems Mart – all three floors of it. The museum contains many magnificent specimens and is well worth a visit if you are interested in finding out more about mining. You will be provided with a locker for your personal belongings, including camera – photography is not allowed.

N.B. On the topic of learning about mining, please be aware that tourists are strongly advised not to go to any mine without first checking with the Ministry of Hotels and Tourism that it is listed as permitted to visit. Going to a mine that you are not authorised to visit could have extremely serious consequences.

Option 6: buying at auction
This is currently only an option for gem traders – tourists and foreigners are not permitted to attend. Twice a year, an auction is organized by the government in Yangon of Myanmar's most beautiful jades and precious stones. The auction lasts for 10 days and people are given 4 days to bid. To enter the auction, you need a special invitation and pay a $100 entrance fee. Myanmar nationals have to pay 30,000 kyats to enter the emporium hall.

Option 7: buying on recommendations
A personal recommendation from people you trust is a powerful thing. If you have friends, colleagues or contacts in Myanmar, use them. You can also use the contacts I have listed in this book. They are there for a reason – because I have met and personally vetted them. No money has changed hands for this recommendation. It's all based on trust!

Useful Burmese words:

Ring	Leth sut
Necklace	Lel shwel
Pendant	Shwel thee
Gold	Shwe
Rough stone	A yai
Cut & polished stone	A chaw

Q&A's

How do I make a complaint?
In Myanmar, there is no official complaint route. Most of the jewellers are reliable and sell stones with a proper lab certificate.

But if a tourist has a complaint/problem, who do they go to?
If you have a complaint against a trader within the Emporium in Yangon, make your complaint to the Government office in the museum. The Gems Museum and Emporium in Yangon is controlled by the government. Contact the Head of the Gems Museum. Traders in the Emporium have to promise to sell only stones from Myanmar. They are obliged to tell tourists the truth and be transparent about whether a gemstone has had any treatment.

How do I make a complaint about a trader outside the Yangon Gems Museum?
It depends on the business – whether or not they are a responsible jeweller. The seller must take the responsibility. Reputation is important – the traders know each other and whether their fellow traders are doing things the right way or the wrong way. Scams are bad for everyone's business.

What happens if a tourist gets home and discovers they've been sold an imitation or glass-filled gemstone?
They would have to communicate with the seller. Some shops will only refund you 90% because they will have already paid the 10% tax due.
Note: Refunds can only be given for a gemstone if you have not had it recut. Once you recut it, the weight will have changed.

At a glance tips

- You can haggle in a gem market, but prices are non-negotiable in a high-end shop.

- If you are buying from the market, negotiate a price and then ask them to provide a lab certificate before you exchange any money.

- Check that the gem has been well cut. Avoid unevenly cut gems and those with a large window. Gems that have been badly cut lose their value and don't look good once set.

- Black pearls do not come from Myanmar!

- Ask for the government receipt cash memo. You'll need this to go through customs at the airport.

- In Myanmar, treating a gemstone is believed to be bad luck, so the chances of getting a heat-treated or glass-filled gemstone are much lower here.

- Look for the sign on a gem shop that says 'Government Licensed'. Government licensed gem shops are not allowed to sell fake gemstones.

- White colourless sapphire is rare to find in Mogok. Check your list of simulants.

REPUTABLE TRADERS IN MYANMAR

From Chan Thar Gyi Pagoda - studded with gemstones and donated by the local people © *Kim Rix*

Yangon

The scope of this book includes Mandalay, Yangon and Mogok

Yangon is known as the *Garden of the East* thanks to its picturesque lakes, parks and tropical trees. A short flight (or day's drive) from Mandalay, Yangon has earned a reputation as the centre of the gem trade in Myanmar and is also famous for its gold.

There is plenty to see and do in Yangon, besides gemstone shopping. The Shwedagon Pagoda, west of the Royal Lake on Singuttara Hill, is one of the world's most sacred and jaw-droppingly impressive Buddhist sites. It houses holy relics, including strands of Buddha's hair, and is covered with hundreds of gold plates. The top of the stupa is encrusted with no fewer than 4531 diamonds, the largest of which is a staggering 72 carats.

The Shwedagon Pagoda © Kim Rix

Yangon boasts a wide range of reputable gem shops, so it's a good place to buy ready-made jewellery. On the other hand, if you would prefer to buy a cut and polished gemstone to make your own piece of jewellery, you have other options besides buying from a shop.

In Yangon, the main areas for trading gemstones and jewellery are:

Myanmar Gem Trade Centre: A government-owned building with four floors, the first three of which are full of licensed shops selling gemstones and jewellery. The fourth floor houses the government office and a gemstone museum.

Bogyoke Aung San Market: An indoor bazaar selling all sorts of crafts, food, clothing, gemstones and jewellery. You'll also find a couple of gem labs here.

Shwe Bon Thar St: This area is mostly for trading gold and currency. The end of this road is crowded with people at small tables, sitting, chatting and trading gemstones. Head here between 9.30am and midday, as traders set up here early in the day and move to Bogyoke market in the afternoon.

Getting there: From the south-west corner of Bogyoke Market, cross the footbridge over the Bogyoke Aung San Road and turn left. Shwe Bon Thar Street is the third on your right. Walk to the very end. For the first 100 yards, you'll pass bookshops, opticians and signage. Go straight over the crossroads and continue for another 100 yards. You will soon see gold shops start to appear. You will also see a few gemstones, but beware, these little gem traders are probably not licensed and are probably selling fakes and imitations. Remember, if it looks too good to be true, it probably is.

Reputable jewellery and gem shops in Yangon

Naing Family Gems & Jewellery Co., Ltd
Contact: Dr Hein Naing Oo, Director
Address: 127D (1-B), Old Yay Tar Shay Road, Bahan Township
By appointment only
Telephone: + 95 9 5189817
Email: naingfamily.mogok@gmail.com

Ayawaddy Jewellery
Contact: Mr Gopal – Nawarat ring Specialist
Address: No.50, East C Block, Bogyoke Aung San Market
Phone: +95 9 73097308
Phone: +95 9 777555510
Email: mrgopal.2012@gmail.com

Brilliant Gems & Jewellery
Contact: Adee Kumar
Address: No. 97, Narawat Hall, 1st Floor, Bogyoke Aung San Market
Email: dhuri.gem@gmail.com
Phone: +95 9 73037263

Gems Palace
Contact: Daw Yin Nwet Thein
Address: No. 51, Narawat (EFG Building), Bogyoke Aung San Market
Phone: +95 1 519790
Email: yinnwet111@gmail.com

Royal jewellery & Jade Handicrafts
Contact: Kaung Naing
Address: Room E-4, Ground Floor, Myanmar Gem Trade Centre, 66 Kabaraye Pagoda Road, Mayangone Township
Phone: +95 9 73154299
Email: kaungnaing82@gmail.com

Jade Carving & Jewellery
Contact: Aung OO Maw
Address: No. 34, 2nd floor, Myanmar Gems Museum
Phone: +95 9 5090932

Special Jewellery
Contact: Mra & Khaing
Address: Counter 7, ground floor,
Myanmar Gems Museum & Gems Mart,
66 Kabaraye Pagoda Road, Mayangone Township
Phone: +95 9 5113539
Phone: +95 9 5107495
Email: mrathida@gmail.com

Forever Gems by Golden Palace
Contact: Dr Aung Kyaw Win, Chairman and Founder
Facebook: Forever Gems by Golden Palace Gold & Jewellery

Fine Gems & Jewellery
Contact: Ye Lwin & Khin Moht Moht
Address: No. 68, Room B-7, Gems Museum & Mart
Myanmar Gems Trade Center, Kabaraye Pagoda Road, Mayangone Township
Phone: +95 9 5014142
Email: mohtmoht16@gmail.com

REPUTABLE TRADERS IN MYANMAR

© Kim Rix

Top Shine Jewellery
Contact: Nang Aue Pyone
Address: No 26, Nawarat Hall, Bogyoke Aung San Market
Phone: +95 9 5049232

Tun Tun Jewellery
Specialises in gold
Address: No 228/230 Shwe Bon Thar Street (Middle block), Pabedan Township
Phone: +95 9 5169550

© Kim Rix

Reputable jewellery and gem shops in Yangon

Bogyoke Aung San Market

Housed in a large, colonial-era building, the Bogyoke Aung San covered market contains over 2000 stalls, selling everything from traditional foods, clothes and crafts to gemstones and fine jewellery. You'll find both expensive gemstones like jade, ruby and sapphire along with cheaper options such as spinel, tourmaline and moonstone.

Location: Bogyoke Aung San Road, Pabedan Township
Selling: 99% cut and polished stones
Open: 9am to 5pm. Closed on Mondays

Bogyoke indoor market, Yangon © *Kim Rix*

REPUTABLE TRADERS IN MYANMAR

Bogyoke indoor market, Yangon © *Kim Rix*

Shops to look out for in Bogyoke Market:

Gems Palace: (ground floor). This shop specialises in jade carvings, but also offers a selection of loose, polished stones. The owner, Yin Nwet, has very few pieces of rough. Visa and MasterCard accepted.
Top Shine Jewellery: (ground floor). Nang Ayeamon has been running the family business for 15 years. The shop offers jade bangles, carvings, earrings and necklaces.
Brilliant Gems and Jewellery: (upstairs). A knowledgeable and friendly business.

Gemstone museums in Yangon

Myanmar Gems Museum & Gems Mart, Yangon

The government-owned Myanmar Gems Museum is located on the top floor of the Gems Mart building on Kaba Aye Pagoda Road and has been running since 1995. Occupying a single room divided into different sections, the museum showcases only 30 of the 100 or so gemstones that can be found in Myanmar. Nevertheless, there is still plenty for gemstone enthusiasts to admire, including cut, rough and gemstones in the matrix, along with displays of jewellery, carvings and pillars entirely made of jade.

Visitor's pass © Kim Rix

You will be given a visitor's pass to wear around your neck.

There are toilets at the back of each floor and a lift for disability access. As well as the museum, the top floor also houses the government office, where you can report any problems with purchases made in the building.

Address: No 66, Kaba Aye Pagoda Road, Mayangone Township
Phone: +95 1 665115
Open: 9.30am to 4pm. Closed Mondays and government holidays.
Entrance fee: $US 5 for foreigners (6800 kyats) and 1000 kyats for locals. Cash only.
Rules: You must sign the guest book and wear a pass.
No photography. No mobile phones
Parking: onsite car park

The world's largest jadeite boulder © Kim Rix

The Gems Mart, Yangon
The Gems Mart occupies floors 1-3 of the same building as the Gems Museum. Spread over these three floors are over 40 shops, offering something for everyone. From the sophisticated buyer who is particular about the design of their gem carving to the first-time buyer looking for a great gift for friends and family, the Gem Mart has plenty of quality carvings or loose stones for you to choose from.

For those who want to buy a gemstone in Myanmar but are worried about fakes, the Gems Mart is a good place to shop. It is government owned and any issues with purchases can be reported at the government office on the fourth floor.

Fine Gems and Jewellery has traded at the Gems Mart for over 3 years and has gained a well-deserved reputation from tourists and locals alike for clearly identifying exactly what they are selling.

Jewellery shows

The Yangon Gems and Jewellery Fair takes place annually in January/February (see website for details). Entry is free of charge and tourists are allowed to attend. Exhibitors at the fair are only permitted to sell natural stone – no synthetics or heavily treated gemstones here! During jewellery show times, there is no limit to what you can buy – foreign visitors can spend millions, even billions, if they wish. Customs officers attending the fair will officially seal up your purchases so you can take them away from the fair and through the airport without further red tape.

Web: www.yangongemsjewelryfair.com

Gem testing laboratories in Yangon

AGGL (Asia Glory Gemmological Laboratory)
The most reputable lab in Yangon.
Address: Room (066) Level 2, Junction City Mall, Corner of Bogyoke Aung San Road and Shwe Dagon Pagoda Road
Phone: +95 9 5177531
Email: aggl.kyawswar@gmail.com
Web: www.aggl-gemlab.com

YGIL (Yangon Gemological Institute and Laboratory)
Contact: Myo Naing, Graduate Gemmologist (GIA)
Address: Room 18, North Wing (Upper floor) Bogyoke Aung San Market, Pabedan Township
Phone: +95 9 5108125

FGA (Standard Gemmological Laboratory)
Contact: Kyaw Wunna, Chief Gemmologist
Address: No. 12, North Wing (Upper floor) Bogyoke Aung San Market, Pabedan Township
Phone: +95 9 787818187
Email: info@fgagemlabmyanmar.com
Web: www.fgagemlabmyanmar.com

GIM (Gemmological Institute of Myanmar)
Training School
Address: 06-07/06-08, Junction City Office Tower, Bogyoke Aung San Road
Email: info@gi-myanmar.org
Web: www.gi-myanmar.org

Stalwart Gem Lab
Address: Room 1, 1st floor, Bogyoke Aung San Market, Pabedan Township
Phone: +95 9 421138287

Travelling around Yangon

Contact: Mg Mg Oo (pronounced Mama Oo)
A friendly and reliable Chinese-born, English speaking taxi driver
Phone: +95 9 791796448
Phone: +95 9 493115902

Mogok Valley of Myanmar, Travels & tours
Contact: Dr Hein Naing Oo
Address: B(12), R(24), Shwegonyeikmon, Bahan Township
Email: mvoyagesm.travels@gmail.com
Phone: +95 9 5189817
Web: www.mvmtravelmyanmar.com

Assessing and marking the jade for cutting © Kim Rix

Mandalay

Mandalay's original name, Yardanarbon, means 'lots of jewels' and you'll certainly find that the city lives up to this description. Mandalay is also justifiably famous for its gold leaf workshops.

The second largest city in Myanmar after Yangon, Mandalay is seen as the country's cultural and religious centre. If you need a break from shopping, famous sites include U Bein Bridge (the world's longest teak bridge), the reconstructed Mandalay Palace and over 700 pagodas. Don't miss UNESCO heritage site Kuthodaw Paya – known as 'the world's biggest book', this Buddhist temple contains 729 marble shrines, each containing a slab inscribed with text from the Buddhist scriptures.

The two main places in Mandalay to buy gemstones and jewellery are the jade market and the Yatana Mall, a shopping centre (appropriately enough, 'yatana' means 'treasures' in Burmese).

Other places of interest: Aung Nan Myanmar Handicrafts Workshop, Shwe Sin Tai Silk House, Mingon Bell Pagoda, the Pagoda on Sagaing Hill and the world's first Jade Pagoda.

Reputable jewellery and gem shops in Mandalay

Kyawt Shin Yadanar Co, Ltd
Specialises in Pearls & Gold
Contact: Khin Nilar Ktaw (MD)
Address: 2nd floor, No. A36, 34th St & 78th corner, Yatanar Mall
Email: nilarkyawtshin68@gmail.com
Phone: +95 9 256066374

Kyawt Shin Yadanar © Kim Rix

The Mingon Bell © *Kim Rix*

Silver Sky Handicraft
Contact: U Ba Mhin and Daw Khin Lay Family
Address: Ywahtaung, Sagaing
Phone: +95 9 43114866
Email: ubamhinsilverware@gmail.com
Web: www.ubamhinsilverware.com

MOE Gems & Jewellery
Contact: Mar Lar Min
Stones are cut and polished in Mogok; the jewellery workshop is in Mandalay.
Address: No 56 (f), 71st Street, between 28th & 29th street
Phone: +95 2 4031775
Email: mtslcl@gmail.com

MOE Gems & Jewellery © Kim Rix

A trader at the Jade Market
Contact: Ko Nyein Kaung, Owner
Address: this shop is located on the north side of the Jade Market and is tricky to find. It is best to get a local guide to call the owner in advance so he can direct you. Unfortunately, the seller does not speak English, so it's best to go with a guide who can translate.
Phone: +95 9 794461040

BUYING GEMSTONES AND JEWELLERY IN **MYANMAR (Burma)**

Kuthodaw Paya, known as 'the world's biggest book' © Kim Rix

King Galon Gold Leaf Workshop
Address: No. 143, 36th St, Between 77th and 78th St, Myet-Parr-Yart

 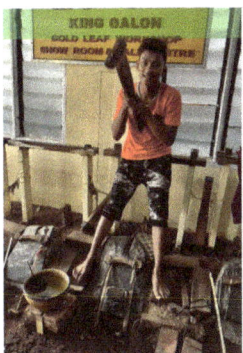 

Watch how gold leaf is made at the King Galon Gold Leaf Workshop © Kim Rix

Aung Nan Myanmar Handicrafts Workshop
Address: No. 97-99 Mandalay-Sagaing Bypass Road, Opposite the Myohaung Warehouse, Pyitawthar Quarter, Chanmyathazi Township
Phone: +95 9 33113500
Email: umu@aungnan.com
Web: www.aungnan.com

Woman embroidering at Aung Nan Myanmar Handicrafts Workshop © Kim Rix

Shwe Sin Tai Silk House © Kim Rix

Shwe Sin Tai Silk House
Contact: Thandar Kyaw, Director
Address: Maung Dan Quarter, Amarapura Township
Phone: +95 9 2001596

Gemstone markets in Mandalay

The jade market

Mandalay's jade market is located in the centre of the town, between 87th and 88th Street and between 38th and 39th street and is where up to 40,000 buyers and sellers congregate daily to deal in Burmese jade. The market's clientele is a mixture of locals and foreigners, with the vast majority of jade being sold to Chinese buyers.

At the jade market © Kim Rix

There are two entrance gates (Eastern Gate and Western Gate) to the jade market. Foreigners will need to pay an entrance fee of around 2500 kyat at a little office to the right of the entrance.

Car parking in the surrounding area is difficult and you'll be lucky to find a space among the two or three thousand motorbikes parked in the street outside each entrance. It's probably best to get a taxi.

The market itself is like a maze – it's fascinating, but easy to lose your sense of direction! If you're interested in learning about jade jewellery production, you'll see many craftspeople cutting & polishing the jade that arrives in large boulders at the market. Some still polish using a traditional bamboo lathe with sand and water. You might come across people grabbing a nap in little nooks and crannies, and there's even a room for playing game of pool.

Don't fancy going into the market? Walk along 39th Street, where you'll find plenty of traders with their stalls laid out on the ground.

Open: 4am to 5pm, daily (closed on full moon and new moon days). The best time to visit is between 7am and 11am.

Gem lab in Mandalay

BGL (Burma Gemological Laboratory)
Opened by a former student and employee of AGGL in Yangon. Most traders who have a shop in the Mandalay Jewellery Mall use BGL.

Address: Room No.A-30, Second floor, Mandalay Yadanabon Super Centre, Between 33/34 Street & 77/78 Street, Chan Aye Thar Zan Township
Open: 10am to 9pm daily
Phone: +95 9 421077778
Email: burmagemlab@gmail.com

Travelling around Mandalay

Contact: Ko Soe Aung
A safe, friendly, local tuk tuk driver
Phone: +95 9 401 603 124

Contact: Mg C (Known as 'Mousey')
A very knowledgeable and personable Burmese, English speaking driver and chauffeur guide
Phone: +95 9 75675257

BUYING GEMSTONES AND JEWELLERY IN **MYANMAR (Burma)**

Kim Rix GG (GIA)

REPUTABLE TRADERS IN MYANMAR

Mogok

View over East Mogok © *Kim Rix*

Mogok, known as 'The Valley of the Rubies', is unique in the history of gem mining for the number and quality of gemstones extracted from its deposits over the years. Documents dating back to the 16th century provide proof of Mogok's gem mining past, though it is estimated that gemstone mining and trading took place in the area as early as the 6th century.

As well as its famous rubies, Mogok produces a plethora of other well-known gemstones, including sapphire, spinel, amber, quartz, spessartite garnet, topaz, tourmaline, lapis lazuli, peridot and moonstone. In fact, almost all gemstones are found in the Mogok tract, with two notable exceptions: emerald and jade.

The tourist trade is still very much in its infancy here, as Mogok was only opened up to tourists in 2018. This means that Mogok is one of the few places that visitors can have a truly authentic experience. Today, 75% of local residents work in the city's mining and gem trading industry and their livelihoods depend on the continued mining, trading, cutting and polishing of gemstones. You won't find gem museums or high street jewellery shops in Mogok, though – most of the trading here is done at the town's four markets. The interactive experience you will get at these markets rivals any museum for learning about the area's gemstones.

Almost all mining in Mogok is still done by hand, with picks and shovels in makeshift shafts 100 metres deep. Miners wearing headtorches bring up buckets of soil and gravel to wash and sift in muddy pools.

Rubies are definitely the star attraction in Mogok. However, the town has much to offer a visitor besides gemstones: breathtaking scenery, local culinary delights and many stunning temples and pagodas, studded with gemstones and gold.

Gem dealers of Mogok

Gem dealers in Mogok proudly say that they are different from other dealers around the world. For many years, they have traded amongst themselves and their relationships have been built on trust. This is why, even today, dealers here are not accustomed to providing certificates for gemstones.

BUYING GEMSTONES AND JEWELLERY IN **MYANMAR (Burma)**

REPUTABLE TRADERS IN MYANMAR

It's difficult to identify the price point at which a Mogok dealer will give you a certificate with your gemstone. At the gem markets, it's a matter of negotiation and you are unlikely to get a certificate for a purchase less than 100 US dollars. Each trader will assess the situation independently. There is no right answer but don't let that stop you from asking.

Gemstone markets in Mogok

There are four main gemstone markets in Mogok, all operating 7 days a week at different times. Mogok's markets are very different from each other.

East Mogok gem markets

Mani Mingalar Market
(formerly the Cinema Market until 2018)
Open: 9am to 12 noon
This morning market takes place near the lake in eastern Mogok and sells low-price souvenirs along with rough and polished gemstones (mostly the latter) varying in price from high to low. This half-day market also has a local name *htar pwe* which means 'tray market'.

Umbrella Market © *Kim Rix*

Panchan market (also known as the Umbrella Market)
Open: 1.30pm to 4.30pm
Entrance fee: tourists pay 1000 kyat to enter the high-end part of the market; locals 100 kyat. Guides go free.

REPUTABLE TRADERS IN MYANMAR

Mani Mingalar Market, the main gems market in Mogok © Kim Rix

Panchan market is held in Pate Swal Quarter and is nicknamed the 'Umbrella Market' because of the umbrellas provided to shade buyers and sellers from the sun. It's Mogok's main market and prices here are not cheap – this market is for the big buyers.

Most of the gemstones sold here are faceted and come with a high price tag. Buyers sit at the tables provided and wait for sellers to approach them. You will usually be shown a mix of rough and polished stones.

West Mogok gem markets

Aung Thit Lwin market (Lan Sone Market)
Open: 9am to 12 noon
The morning gem market has two names. Aung Thit Lwin market is its official name, but people know it as Lan Sone market – which means 'Junction' market.

At this market there are no tables and all trading is done standing. Predominantly this market is where people sell polished stones but you will find some rough.

Aung Thit Lwin market © *Kim Rix*

Pan Ma market
Open: 4pm to 5.30pm (evening market)
Here you will find mostly rough but some cut & polished gemstones on offer and trading is done standing. The gemstones here are in the lower price ranges.

Tha Phan Pin market
Open: 9am to 12 noon
Ruby is the only gemstone sold at this market.

Reputable jewellery and gem shops in East Mogok

Contact: Mr U Kyaw Naing & Mrs Daw Zin Mar Oo
A private family business specialising in medium to high-end quality Mogok rubies and sapphires
Address: No. 118 Bogyoke St, Myoma Quarter
By appointment only
Phone: +95 9 797777994

A very busy Pan Ma market © Kim Rix

Ko Top Sone Jewellery
This jewellery-making workshop specialises in gold. Choose your design from an extensive catalogue or ask them to create a bespoke piece for you. A very professional and friendly family-run business.
Address: Htinn Shu Chan Quarter, Mogok City
Phone: +95 9 400004474
Phone: +95 0 788788588

Million Gold, Jewellery & Monk Robe

Guarded by security, this marketplace has a few gold shops. Million Gold has good high-end jewellery, including Mogok ruby and sapphire pendants.
Contact: Ko Pyae Kyaw + Ma Nang May Thingyan Htwe
Address: Aung Chan Tar Quarter, Ruby Market No C 2, 4, 6, 8, 10
Telephone: +95 9 402 524 666

Gem labs in East Mogok

International Gemological Research Laboratory
Contact: Kay Khine Thwin, Senior Gemmologist
Address: No. 118 Bogyoke St, Myoma Quarter
By appointment only
Phone: +95 9 797777994
Email: info@IGRL-GEMLAB.com

Ruby pendant by Million Gold, Jewellery & Monk Robe © Kim Rix

U Kyaw Laboratory
Address: 77 Mya Seinn Yaung Road, Sittan Quarter
Phone: +95 9 402724404
Note that this lab has gained a reputation for charging high prices!

Lilanath
Address: 249 Aung Chan Thar
Phone: +95 9 402524616

This laboratory, situated very close to the Zaykalay produce market, is the most popular lab in Mogok. Certificate prices depend on several factors, including the type of gemstone, its size and whether the certificate includes a photo. The average price to get a gemstone tested is 5000 kyat per gemstone (a few USD dollars).

Mogok Gemstone Paintings

There are some incredibly skilled artists in Mogok making gemstone paintings, a traditional and sustainable form of artwork that uses genuine gemstone material left over from the cutting process to make pictures. Gemstone paintings make great souvenirs and enable many artists to feed their families.

In Mogok, the gem paintings are made on whiteboard or wood, about 3-4 mm thick. The artist begins by carefully drawing the outlines of the piece on the board. These outlines are then filled in with gemstone powder – some very fine, like sand, and some coarser, like breadcrumbs. The Mogok style of gem art uses a combination of gemstone powder with brush painting.

If you're tempted, get the painting wrapped up at the workshop and pack it carefully in your suitcase. If your painting is too big to fit in your case, you should be able to carry it with you on the plane – a bit of fast talking and charm at the airport might help you avoid an extra check-in charge!

REPUTABLE TRADERS IN MYANMAR

Mogok Gem Painting Workshop
Contact: U Win Myint and Daw Cho Mar
Address: No.163, Below Lal Oo Quarter

Watch gem paintings being made in Mogok © *Kim Rix*

Rubies being set in a ring. Top Sone jewellery workshop © *Kim Rix*

REPUTABLE TRADERS IN MYANMAR

BUYING GEMSTONES AND JEWELLERY IN **MYANMAR (Burma)**

At the mine in Mogok © Kim Rix

ESSENTIAL INFORMATION

Mine shaft © *Kim Rix*

ESSENTIAL INFORMATION

Visas and permits

Visa to enter Myanmar

Most foreign nationals require a visa to enter Myanmar. Check your visa status here: https://www.go-myanmar.com/visas

Permission papers to visit Mogok

Tourists and visitors who want to enter Mogok must have official permission and the paperwork to prove it. Permission papers are granted by the government and can be arranged through your travel agent. They will need passport and visa details to apply on your behalf. Permission papers cost $50 US.

Three hours from Mandalay – the immigration point for entering Mogok © Kim Rix

Mandatory tour guide to visit Mogok

Foreigners are not allowed to travel alone in Mogok. Since Mogok has only recently been opened up to visitors, the laws relating to what foreigners can and cannot do are still in a state of flux.

Some mining areas are still off limits to tourists and are closely patrolled by the military. Those found trespassing could find themselves in serious hot water, and therefore the law states that foreigners in Mogok must be accompanied by a tour guide. Tour guides can be arranged by your travel agent.

Travelling around Mogok

Jordan July
A well-known, knowledgeable, local expert. Offers travel services for tourists.
Phone: +95 942 653 8464
Email: 19jordan@gmail.com

Top Tip: it is not customary and there is no pressure to tip in Myanmar, but cash tips are certainly appreciated by tour drivers and guides.

ESSENTIAL INFORMATION

Certificates of authenticity and grading reports

The value of a gemstone depends on several factors, some of which you read about in the chapter 'Knowing what you're looking at'. At its most basic, the rule of thumb is this: the rarer, the bigger and the more naturally beautiful a gemstone is, the more it will be worth. The problem is that you cannot fully analyse a stone with the naked eye or gemmologist's loupe (magnifying glass).

This is where the gem labs come in. In a gem lab, experts using high-tech equipment will be able to give you a lot of information about your stone. How much information you get depends on whether you want a certificate of authenticity or a grading report.

Certificate of authenticity

A certificate of authenticity is a written guarantee that your gemstone is what the seller says it is. It does not contain much specific detail about the stone. A certificate is really there to reassure you that you're getting a genuine gemstone and not a chunk of glass. Many gems, especially those bought in shops, hotels or museums, will be sold with such a certificate.

Whether or not this is a genuine certificate, is another matter. It's very easy to create a certificate of authenticity simply by downloading a template from the internet. Ultimately, you will have to use your own judgement about the respectability of the establishment, but there are measures you can take to ensure you really are getting a genuine stone. One is to call the establishment or body listed on the certificate and check the certificate number with them. The **safest** measure, however, is simply to get the gem examined and certified by a lab **before you buy**. A reputable establishment should be happy to accompany you to a lab for this purpose.

www.gemstonedetective.com

Grading report

A grading report gives a **detailed analysis** of a gemstone. It will provide you with a written assessment of your gemstone according to several criteria: carat weight, shape, size, colour description, clarity, and the type of treatment it has undergone. A grading report can also tell you your gemstone's country of origin. This can have a bearing on the value of the gemstone because some countries have become associated with the quality of particular stones. For example, a Burmese ruby will fetch more than an otherwise equivalent ruby from Mozambique, Thailand or Tanzania. Note that testing for origin can only be carried out on loose stones. If the gemstone has already been set into a piece of jewellery, it will need to be removed and then re-set after the test.

Here is an example:

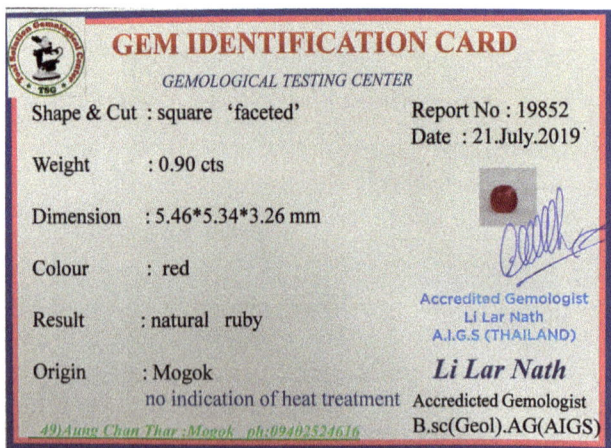

ESSENTIAL INFORMATION

Before you take your gemstone for testing, though, you need to be aware of the following caveats:

- Laboratories certify gemstones, but **no one certifies laboratories**. Gem labs stand on their reputation alone.

- There is **no standard method for testing gemstones.** Each lab will have its own process and so it is possible that the same gemstone, tested at different labs, could come back with very different reports.

- **Beware of labs issuing grading reports which are in fact certificates/appraisals.** A full grading report will include an assessment of the origin, colour, clarity, treatments and the final quality grading of your gemstone. Note that testing the origin of your gemstone may mean paying an additional fee.

- Always **check that the lab name on your report is the same all the way through the document.** The cover on your report might come from well-known and established lab, but the pages inside from a lab with a very slightly altered name. Sometimes the difference is very subtle.

BUYING GEMSTONES AND JEWELLERY IN **MYANMAR (Burma)**

ESSENTIAL INFORMATION

Prices – what to expect

Gem prices fluctuate year on year and depend on the origin, colour, clarity, cut and carat weight of each individual gemstone.

Burmese gemstones are famed for being some of the best in the world. This is reflected in the prices you'll be quoted. You will find prices are unrealistically high in Myanmar, particularly in Mogok. However, it is still very much worth trying to agree a lower price if you are prepared to negotiate hard. Do some research to get an idea of realistic prices and decide what you are prepared to pay.

If you are planning to spend a lot, make sure that you have the gemstone tested before you exchange any money. Cash (local currency, fresh bank notes) is the preferred method of payment at the gem market.

Natural, unheated peridot, mined in Mogok © *Kim Rix*

Gemstones as investments

Is it a good idea to buy a Burmese gemstone as a part of your retirement plan? There is no simple answer to this question and you should bear in mind that all investments involve some degree of risk. That said, a diversified portfolio carries less risk than putting all of your eggs in one basket, so why not include a precious gemstone or two alongside your other assets?

Gemstones are hard assets. Historically, they have been seen as a hedge against inflation and the breakdown of more abstract forms of investment such as stocks and bonds.

Gemstones do increase in value, but it's a long-term game. Gemstone prices fluctuate, like any investment. Over the long term, however, gemstones have risen in value significantly. Nevertheless, be aware that they will not be as easy to liquidate as other assets, should you need cash in a hurry!

With all this in mind, if you wish to buy a Burmese gemstone as an investment, buy only the best quality. I strongly recommend that you also seek the advice of a neutral professional before you part with large amounts of money.

The ethics of buying gemstones

These days, tourists are thankfully more aware of the ethical issues that dog the gemstone industry. Almost everybody has heard of conflict (or 'blood') diamonds, mined and sold in war zones to fund the carnage of civil war. Human-rights abuses and the environmental impact of large-scale mining are things that should be foremost in our minds when buying gemstones at home and abroad. We need to know that our business is supporting rather than exploiting people.

On my travels, I have met and come to know many people who depend on artisanal mining to support their families. It's these small businesses that really suffer from lack of confidence in the gem trade. If we stop buying from the small-scale mines, livelihoods are destroyed. When abroad, I have made it my mission to build long-term relationships with people I trust – people who are doing the right thing by their workers and their environment.

APPENDICES

Glossary

Adularescence   An optical effect that makes a gemstone appear to glow from within. Moonstones exhibit adularescence

Allochromatic   Describes a gemstone whose colour is caused by impurities or defects in its chemical structure

Asterism   An optical effect in which a four, six or twelve rayed star appears to float just beneath the surface of the gem. Gemstones exhibiting asterism are given the name 'star'

Brilliance   The 'flashing' effect produced by light entering the stone and bouncing off its interior facets. Only transparent stones can be said to have brilliance

Carat   The unit used to measure the weight of a gemstone

Certificate   Confirmation that the gem in question is authentic

Chatoyancy   An optical effect in which a straight line appears to float just beneath the surface of the gem. Gemstones exhibiting chatoyancy are called 'cat's eye' stones.

Clarity   The quality of transparency of a gemstone

Corundum   A very hard, transparent mineral. Ruby and sapphire are colour variations of corundum

APPENDICES

Cutting	The process of shaping and polishing a rough stone
Faceting	Cutting
Fire	The tendency of a stone's structure to split white light into the colours of the rainbow. Diamond is famous for this
Fluorescence	The ability of a gemstone to absorb ultraviolet light and emit it as visible light.
Grading report	A detailed analysis of a gemstone's quality
Heat treatment	A very old traditional method of improving the clarity of a gemstone. Not all gems can be treated in this way, but most sapphires are.
Hue	The colour of a stone
Idiochromatic	Describes a gemstone whose colour is due to its chemical composition rather than an impurity.
Imitation	A stone that imitates a more expensive stone. An imitation stone might be a less valuable semi-precious stone, or it might simply be coloured glass.
Inclusion	A fleck of material within a stone. A flaw
Loupe	A small magnifying glass used to examine gems
Lustre	The 'gleam' produced by light bouncing off the surface of a stone

Metamorphic	Has undergone a physical change due to extreme heat and pressure
Pleochroic	Describes a gemstone whose colour appears to change when viewed from different angles
Refractive index	A measure of the change in the speed and direction of light as it passes through a material
Rough stone	A natural gemstone before it has been cut, or 'faceted'
Saturation	The intensity of colour in a gemstone
Simulant	A cheap gemstone trying to look like a more valuable one
Synthetic	A gemstone identical in structure to a mined gemstone, but formed in a lab rather than naturally in the earth
Tone	How light or dark a gemstone appears to be
Window	An area within a gemstone that does not reflect light and therefore appears flat and dull. It's called a window because you can see through it

APPENDICES

Acknowledgements

My sincere thanks go to the following people, who were involved in the chain of events that made this book possible:

First of all, my publisher Chris Day who put me in touch with published author, Feroze Dada FCA, CTA of the Inle Trust. Feroze Dada put me in touch with Brig General Tin Maung Swe of the Burma Embassy in London. Brig General Tin Maung Swe introduced me to U Khin Maung in Yangon, who kindly met with me and connected me with the Myanmar Gems & Jewellery Entrepreneurs Association.

My sincere thanks to The Board of the Myanmar Gems & Jewellery Entrepreneurs Association for sharing their time and knowledge:
Dr Aung Kyaw Win, Vice Chairman, Mrs Mying Thet Naing, Vice Chairman, Nyunt Nyunt Khine, Joint Treasurer, Mra & Kaing, Aung Oo Maw.

Image - from Left to right: U Kaung Naing, U Than Maung, Dr Aung Kyaw Win, Kim Rix, Daw Myint Thet Naing and Daw Nyunt Nyunt Khaing

I am grateful to everyone mentioned in this book; without them, there would be no book. They were exceedingly kind, open and generous in sharing their knowledge and I hope that this book will help bring them more business and prosperity.

Special thanks to:

Steven Rix, Nyein Nyein Lwin, Dr Hein Naing Oo, Kay Khine Thwin and Mee Nge

About the author

Kim Rix is a professional photographer and qualified gemmologist (GIA). She travels extensively and has gathered a vast amount of the best local knowledge from her world wide contacts.

Buying Gemstones & Jewellery in Myanmar is the seventh book in the *Gemstone Detective* series. Those interested in arranging speaking engagements may contact the author via the web site: www.gemstonedetective.com or email kim@gemstonedetective.com

Disclaimer: Kim Rix travelled to Myanmar in 2018, 2019 and 2020 to gain insight into the marketplace with the intention of writing this book. Any resulting articles or publications should not be taken or used as an endorsement.

If we have made any errors in this book, please

 Forgive us

 Correct us

 Contact: kim@gemstonedetective.com

APPENDICES

Connect with us

We would love you to leave a review of the book wherever you can – including Amazon, Google, Goodreads and our website.

 www.facebook.com/GemstoneDetective

 www.twitter.com/kimrix

 www.instagram.com/gemstone_detective

You can also sign up to receive our latest news and travels straight to your inbox via the website:

 www.gemstonedetective.com

Groups interested in arranging speaking engagements may contact the author via the website: www.gemstonedetective.com or by email at kim@gemstonedetective.com

Gemstone Tours with *Gemstone Detective* are escorted group tours. We visit the leading sources of colour gemstones, in search of ruby, sapphire, emerald, jade, opal and many others. For more information on booking a Gemstone Tour, please visit www.gemstonedetective.com/gemstone-tours

www.ingramcontent.com/pod-product-compliance
Lightning Source LLC
Chambersburg PA
CBHW041957080526
44588CB00021B/2781